DK

A DK PUBLISHING BOOK

Designer Ingrid Mason
Illustrator Graham Corbett
Picture researcher Sue Wookey
Photography Peter Anderson, Jim Coit,
and Roland Kemp

First American Edition, 1994
4 6 8 10 9 7 5

Published in the United States by
DK Publishing, Inc., 95 Madison Avenue,
New York, New York 10016

ISBN 0-56458-659-6

Reproduced by Colourscan, Singapore
Printed and bound in Italy by L.E.G.O.

1 2 3 4 5 6 7 8 9 10

The
Teddy Bear
Counting Book

DK

1

One big bear,

2

Two make a pair.

3

Three all in brown,

4

Four go to town.

5

Five looking fluffy,

6

Six very scruffy.

7

Seven bears in bows,

8

Eight in two rows.

9

Nine making friends,

10

Ten, that's the end!